"THE AI MILLIONAIRE: NAVIGATING INNOVATION, ETHICAL WEALTH, AND A FUTURE BEYOND PROSPERITY"

"The AI Millionaire"

Dive into a world where innovation meets prosperity in Zohaib Hassan Khan's groundbreaking book, "The AI Millionaire." A visionary entrepreneur and thought leader in artificial intelligence, Khan takes you on a transformative journey through the intersection of cutting-edge technology and unparalleled wealth accumulation.

Uncover the secrets of AI-driven success, where financial prosperity is just the beginning. Khan explores the ethical dimensions, societal impact, and responsibilities that come with being an AI millionaire. This is not just a guide to wealth; it's an invitation to shape the future, leaving a legacy of positive change.

From emerging technologies to the balanced approach of a holistic AI millionaire, this book is your passport to the forefront of the digital age. Join Khan in redefining success, where the power of AI extends beyond balance sheets and into a world where innovation and ethical leadership intertwine.

Are you ready to unleash the future of wealth and become a part of a transformative narrative? "The AI Millionaire" awaits, offering insights, inspiration, and a roadmap to success in the dynamic landscape of artificial intelligence.

Prologue: A Journey beyond Wealth

Dear Reader,

Welcome to a world where innovation meets prosperity, and artificial intelligence becomes the catalyst for unprecedented success. In the pages that follow, I invite you to embark on a transformative journey—"The AI **Millionaire:** Unleashing the Future of Wealth." This is not just a book; it's a roadmap to a future where AI-driven ventures are not only financially lucrative but also pillars of positive change.

As you turn these pages, you'll explore the intersection of artificial intelligence and wealth accumulation, guided by the principles, strategies, and insights shared within. But this book is more than a guide; it's an invitation to envision a future where success transcends balance sheets, and the impact extends far beyond personal gain.

Why This Book?

In an era where technology shapes the destiny of industries and individuals, understanding the dynamics of AI-driven wealth is not just an advantage; it's a necessity. Whether you're an aspiring entrepreneur, an investor navigating the digital landscape, or simply curious about the future, this book offers a unique perspective on leveraging artificial intelligence for transformative success.

What Awaits You?

Innovation Explored: Discover cutting-edge technologies and emerging trends shaping the future of AI wealth.

Entrepreneurial Insights: Gain practical wisdom from real-world examples of AI millionaires who have navigated challenges and achieved extraordinary success.

Ethical Considerations: Delve into the ethical dimensions of AI wealth accumulation, exploring responsible practices and the broader societal impact.

Beyond Financial Success: Uncover the potential for AI millionaires to contribute to social impact, philanthropy, and the well-being of humanity.

Why Now?

The future is unfolding at an unprecedented pace, and your understanding of the AI landscape today will shape your success tomorrow. Whether you're an innovator, a decision-maker, or an enthusiast, now is the time to grasp the possibilities that AI presents and position yourself at the forefront of change.

Are You Ready?

Turn the page. Immerse yourself in a narrative that transcends traditional success stories. "The AI Millionaire" is not just a book; it's an invitation to envision, innovate, and create a future where your wealth becomes a force for positive change.

As we embark on this journey together, I encourage you to open your mind, challenge your perspectives, and embrace the transformative potential of AI-driven wealth. The adventure begins now.

With anticipation and excitement,

Zohaib Hassan Khan

Author, Innovator, AI Enthusiast

Zohaib Hassan Khan: Architect of AI Success

Zohaib Hassan Khan is not merely an author; he is an architect of the future, a trailblazer in the realm where artificial intelligence intersects with unprecedented wealth accumulation. Renowned for his visionary approach to innovation and entrepreneurship, Zohaib has emerged as a thought leader in the dynamic landscape of AI-driven ventures.

Visionary Entrepreneurship

With a background steeped in technology and a keen eye for emerging trends, Zohaib has successfully navigated the intricate pathways of entrepreneurship in the age of artificial intelligence. As the founder and CEO of cutting-edge AI ventures, his strategic insights have not only propelled businesses to financial success but have also set new benchmarks for ethical and sustainable practices in the industry.

Thought Leadership

Zohaib's journey is not just about accumulating wealth; it's a commitment to pioneering change. As a thought leader, he has shared his expertise on global platforms, shaping discussions on the ethical implications of AI, the future of innovation, and the responsibilities that come with success in the digital age.

Mentorship and Education

Beyond his ventures and leadership roles, Zohaib is dedicated to nurturing the next generation of innovators. His commitment to mentorship and education extends to guiding aspiring entrepreneurs, sharing knowledge, and fostering an environment where curiosity and continuous learning thrive.

Philanthropy and Social Impact

Zohaib's vision extends beyond financial success—it encompasses a commitment to social impact and philanthropy. Recognizing the transformative potential of AI for the greater good, he actively engages in initiatives that leverage technology to address societal challenges, promote inclusivity, and contribute to environmental sustainability.

Authorship

"The AI Millionaire: Unleashing the Future of Wealth" is a testament to Zohaib's passion for sharing knowledge and inspiring others to unlock their potential in the world of artificial intelligence. In this book, he distills years of experience, insights, and forward-thinking strategies to guide readers on a journey that goes beyond financial success.

Join the Journey

As you delve into the pages of "The AI Millionaire," consider yourself not only a reader but a companion on a journey led by a visionary author. Zohaib Hassan Khan invites you to explore the future of wealth, innovation, and ethical leadership. Join him on this transformative adventure where success is measured not just in dollars but in positive change and lasting impact.

Table of Contents

Introduction

Different AI investment strategies and applications

Case studies on successful AI-driven investment portfolios

Automated Trading and Wealth Accumulation

In-depth exploration of algorithmic trading

Case studies on wealth accumulation through automation

Role of machine learning in optimizing trading algorithms

Part II: Advanced AI Applications in Wealth Creation

Innovative AI Ventures

Exploration of innovative AI-driven business ventures

Chapter 1: INTRODUCTION TO AI WEALTH

Overview:

In this opening chapter, Zohaib Hassan Khan introduces readers to the fundamental concepts of AI-driven wealth creation. The chapter sets the stage for the entire book by providing an overview of the intersection between artificial intelligence and financial success. It aims to familiarize readers with the book's purpose, structure, and the historical context of AI in the realms of business and finance.

Key Content:

Purpose and Structure of the Book:

Khan articulates the goals and intentions behind "The AI Millionaire." Readers gain insight into what they can expect from the book, its key themes, and how the content is organized.

Historical Context of AI in Business and Finance:

The chapter delves into the historical progression of AI technologies and their integration into the business and financial sectors. This historical perspective helps readers understand the evolution of AI's role in wealth creation.

Evolution of the Relationship between AI and Financial Success:

Khan explores how the relationship between AI and financial success has evolved over time. This includes the initial stages of experimentation, breakthroughs, and the current landscape where AI is considered a pivotal factor in achieving financial prosperity.

Target Audience:

This chapter caters to a broad audience, including individuals with varying levels of familiarity with AI and finance. It is designed to engage both newcomers seeking an introduction to the topic and those with existing knowledge looking for a comprehensive overview.

Chapter Objectives:

To Familiarize Readers: Introduce readers to the concept of AI-driven wealth and its significance in contemporary business and finance.

To Provide Context: Establish a historical context to highlight the journey of AI in contributing to financial success.

To Set Expectations: Outline the structure and purpose of the book, preparing readers for the in-depth exploration of AI's role in wealth creation.

Takeaways:

Readers completing Chapter 1 will have a foundational understanding of the book's overarching themes, the historical trajectory of AI in business, and a sense of the pivotal role AI plays in contemporary financial success.

HOW TO ACCUMALATE AI WELATH;

Accumulating wealth through AI involves leveraging artificial intelligence technologies to make informed decisions, optimize processes, and create value. Here are several strategies to accumulate AI wealth:

Education and Skill Development:

Invest time in learning about AI technologies, machine learning, and data science.

Acquire skills in programming languages like Python, which are commonly used in AI development.

Stay updated on the latest advancements and trends in AI through online courses, workshops, and conferences.

Identifying Opportunities:

Explore industries where AI can bring significant value, such as finance, healthcare, e-commerce, and logistics.

Identify problems or inefficiencies within these industries that AI can address and improve.

Entrepreneurship and Business Ventures:

Consider starting an AI-driven business or integrating AI into an existing venture.

Develop innovative products or services that solve real-world problems using AI technologies.

Investing in AI:

Explore investment opportunities in AI startups or companies that heavily leverage AI in their operations.

Diversify investments across different sectors within the AI ecosystem, such as robotics, natural language processing, or computer vision.

Algorithmic Trading:

Explore automated or algorithmic trading strategies that leverage AI to analyze market trends and make data-driven investment decisions.

Develop or utilize AI-powered trading algorithms to optimize trading performance.

Data Monetization:

Explore ways to monetize data by creating AI models that extract valuable insights.

Consider offering data-driven products or services to businesses looking to leverage AI for decision-making.

AI in Real Estate:

Explore opportunities in the real estate market by using AI for property valuation, demand prediction, or personalized customer experiences.

Consider AI-driven solutions for property management and investment analysis.

Strategic Partnerships and Collaboration:

Collaborate with experts in AI, data science, and related fields to enhance your capabilities.

Form strategic partnerships with AI companies or professionals to leverage their expertise and resources.

Continuous Innovation:

Stay innovative by exploring emerging technologies and incorporating them into your AI strategies.

Embrace a culture of continuous improvement and adaptability to stay ahead in the dynamic field of AI.

Ethical AI Practices:

Prioritize ethical considerations in AI development and usage to build trust with stakeholders.

Demonstrate a commitment to responsible AI practices, transparency, and fairness.

Chapter 2: **THE RISE OF THE AI ENTREPRENEUR**

Overview:

This chapter delves into the inspiring stories of successful AI entrepreneurs, examining how they navigated the evolving landscape of artificial intelligence to build prosperous businesses. Zohaib Hassan Khan explores the entrepreneurial mindset, innovative strategies, and key factors that contributed to their success.

Key Content:

Profiles of Successful AI Entrepreneurs:

In-depth profiles of prominent AI entrepreneurs who have made a significant impact in their respective industries.

Case studies detailing their entrepreneurial journey, challenges faced, and strategies employed.

AI-Driven Business Success:

Analysis of businesses that have thrived by integrating AI into their core operations.

Examination of diverse sectors, including tech, healthcare, finance, and more, showcasing the versatility of AI entrepreneurship.

Entrepreneurial Mindset in the AI Space:

Exploration of the unique mindset required to succeed as an AI entrepreneur.

Insights into risk-taking, innovation, and the ability to adapt to the fast-paced nature of the AI industry.

Impact of AI on Traditional Business Models:

Discussion on how AI has disrupted and transformed traditional business models.

Examples of industries where AI-driven startups have challenged and reshaped established norms.

Opportunities and Challenges for Aspiring AI Entrepreneurs:

Identification of opportunities within the AI ecosystem for aspiring entrepreneurs.

A realistic assessment of challenges and potential pitfalls, along with strategies to overcome them.

Target Audience:

This chapter is tailored for individuals aspiring to become AI entrepreneurs, as well as those interested in understanding the mindset and strategies of successful AI business leaders. It caters to a diverse audience, including business professionals, students, and anyone intrigued by the entrepreneurial aspects of AI.

Chapter Objectives:

Inspiration and Learning: Provide inspiration through the success stories of AI entrepreneurs while offering practical lessons for aspiring business leaders.

Understanding the Landscape: Explore the impact of AI on traditional business models, highlighting opportunities and challenges in the rapidly evolving entrepreneurial landscape.

Mindset Development: Foster an understanding of the entrepreneurial mindset required to navigate the dynamic AI industry successfully.

Takeaways:

Readers completing Chapter 2 will gain insights into the world of AI entrepreneurship, drawing inspiration from real-life success stories. They will understand the transformative impact of AI on traditional business models and be equipped with knowledge to navigate the challenges and opportunities in the AI entrepreneurial space.

Chapter 3: AI INVESTMENT STRATEGIES IN TODAY'S LANDSCAPE

Overview:

This chapter focuses on the contemporary landscape of AI investment strategies, providing readers with insights into the latest advancements and how they can capitalize on AI to achieve financial freedom. Zohaib Hassan Khan guides readers through cutting-edge approaches and technologies shaping the financial markets.

Key Content:

State-of-the-Art AI Investment Technologies:

Exploration of the latest AI-driven tools and technologies reshaping investment strategies in today's dynamic markets.

Discussion on advanced machine learning models, natural language processing, and predictive analytics.

Data-Driven Decision-Making:

Emphasis on the importance of data in AI-driven investment decisions.

How big data and real-time analytics empower investors to make informed choices in a rapidly changing financial landscape.

Algorithmic Trading Revisited:

Updates on the current state of algorithmic trading, with a focus on high-frequency trading, automated execution, and smart order routing.

Case studies illustrating successful algorithmic trading strategies in contemporary markets.

Crypto currencies and AI:

Examination of the intersection between AI and the crypto currency market.

How AI is utilized for price prediction, risk management, and portfolio optimization in the volatile world of crypto currencies.

Robot-Advisors and AI Wealth Management:

Insights into the rise of robot-advisors and AI-driven wealth management platforms.

How individuals can leverage these automated services for hands-off investment management.

Social Media and Sentiment Analysis:

Exploration of how AI is used for sentiment analysis on social media platforms to gauge market sentiment.

The impact of social media data on investment decisions and risk management.

Personalized Financial Planning with AI:

The role of AI in personalized financial planning, including budgeting, savings optimization, and retirement planning.

How individuals can use AI tools to tailor financial strategies to their unique goals and circumstances.

Target Audience:

This chapter is designed for individuals interested in contemporary AI investment strategies, ranging from seasoned investors to those just entering the financial landscape. It caters to a diverse audience, including investors, financial analysts, and anyone seeking to enhance their financial decision-making with AI.

Chapter Objectives:

Stay Current: Provide readers with up-to-date information on the latest AI technologies and their applications in finance.

Practical Applications: Illustrate how individuals can practically apply AI investment strategies to enhance their financial well-being.

Risk Management: Discuss the importance of risk management in AI-driven investments and how individuals can navigate potential challenges.

Takeaways:

Upon completing Chapter 3, readers will gain a deep understanding of how contemporary AI investment strategies can be applied to achieve financial freedom. They will be equipped with insights into cutting-edge technologies and practical approaches to navigate today's financial landscape.

Chapter 4: AI-POWERED ENTREPRENEURSHIP AND BUSINESS GROWTH

Overview:

This chapter explores how individuals can harness the power of artificial intelligence to drive entrepreneurship and achieve substantial business growth. Zohaib Hassan Khan delves into the current landscape of AI applications for business, providing insights into innovative strategies, technologies, and successful case studies.

Key Content:

AI-Driven Innovation in Business:

An overview of how AI is fostering innovation across various industries.

Case studies highlighting businesses that have successfully integrated AI to drive innovation and gain a competitive edge.

Automation and Efficiency:

Exploration of AI-driven automation and its impact on operational efficiency.

Discussion on how businesses can streamline processes, reduce costs, and improve overall productivity through automation.

Customer-Centric AI Solutions:

Insights into the use of AI to enhance customer experiences.

Case studies on businesses leveraging AI-powered catboats, personalization engines, and recommendation systems to cater to individual customer needs.

Predictive Analytics for Business Decision-Making:

Examination of how AI-driven predictive analytics is transforming decision-making in business.

Real-world examples of companies using predictive analytics for market forecasting, demand planning, and strategic decision support.

AI in Marketing and Sales:

How businesses are leveraging AI for targeted marketing campaigns and personalized sales strategies.

The role of AI in lead generation, customer segmentation, and improving conversion rates.

Supply Chain Optimization with AI:

The impact of AI on supply chain management and logistics.

Case studies on businesses optimizing supply chain processes through AI-driven demand forecasting, inventory management, and logistics optimization.

Scaling Businesses with AI:

Strategies for scaling businesses using AI technologies.

Exploration of how AI can contribute to the scalability of startups and established enterprises alike.

Target Audience:

This chapter is tailored for entrepreneurs, business owners, and individuals interested in understanding how AI can be strategically implemented to drive business growth. It caters to a diverse audience, including those involved in various business sectors seeking to gain a competitive advantage through AI.

Chapter Objectives:

Strategic Implementation: Provide insights into strategically implementing AI for business growth.

Practical Applications: Illustrate practical applications of AI in different business domains, offering inspiration for entrepreneurs and business leaders.

Scalability: Discuss how AI can contribute to the scalability of businesses and startups.

Takeaways:

Readers completing Chapter 4 will gain a comprehensive understanding of how AI can be a driving force behind entrepreneurship and business growth. They will be equipped with practical insights, case studies, and strategies to integrate AI into their business models for enhanced efficiency and competitiveness.

1. AI-Driven Innovation in Business

Overview:

This section provides an overview of how AI is serving as a catalyst for innovation across diverse industries. It introduces the concept of AI-driven innovation and sets the stage for the subsequent discussions on its applications in various business contexts.

Case Studies:

Detailed case studies highlighting businesses that have successfully integrated AI to drive innovation.

Examples showcase the transformative impact of AI on product development, service delivery, and overall business models.

2. Automation and Efficiency

Overview:

The focus shifts to the realm of automation powered by AI and its implications for operational efficiency within businesses. This section explores how AI-driven automation is reshaping traditional processes, leading to cost reduction and increased productivity.

Practical Examples:

Concrete examples illustrating how businesses are leveraging AI for automation in areas such as data entry, routine tasks, and backend processes.

Insights into the benefits of AI-driven efficiency, including improved accuracy, reduced turnaround time, and resource optimization.

3. Customer-Centric AI Solutions

Overview:

Examining the application of AI in enhancing customer experiences, this section explores how businesses can leverage AI to cater to individual customer needs. It introduces the concept of customer-centric AI solutions and their impact on brand loyalty and satisfaction.

AI-Powered Tools:

Discussion on AI-powered tools such as catboats, personalization engines, and recommendation systems.

Real-world examples of businesses effectively using these tools to create personalized and seamless customer interactions.

4. Predictive Analytics for Business Decision-Making

Overview:

Shifting the focus to predictive analytics, this section explores how businesses can leverage AI to make informed decisions. It introduces the role of predictive analytics in market forecasting, demand planning, and overall strategic decision-making.

Real-World Examples:

In-depth exploration of real-world examples where predictive analytics has played a crucial role in guiding business decisions.

Illustrations of how businesses have achieved a competitive edge by using AI to analyze data and anticipate future trends.

5. AI in Marketing and Sales

Overview:

This section delves into the application of AI in marketing and sales strategies. It explores how businesses can use AI to optimize marketing campaigns, improve customer targeting, and enhance conversion rates.

Strategies and Implementation:

Strategies for implementing AI in marketing and sales, including personalized marketing, lead generation, and customer segmentation.

Examples showcasing the effectiveness of AI-driven marketing in adapting to changing consumer behaviors.

6. Supply Chain Optimization with AI

Overview:

Highlighting the impact of AI on supply chain management, this section discusses how businesses can optimize processes in logistics, demand forecasting, and inventory management.

Case Studies:

Exploration of case studies demonstrating successful implementations of AI in supply chain optimization.

Insights into how businesses have achieved cost savings, reduced inefficiencies, and enhanced overall supply chain resilience.

7. Scaling Businesses with AI

Overview:

This concluding section focuses on strategies for scaling businesses using AI technologies. It explores how AI can contribute to the scalability of both startups and established enterprises.

Scalability Strategies:

Strategies for leveraging AI in scaling operations, expanding market reach, and handling increased business volumes.

Real-world examples illustrating how businesses have effectively scaled with the integration of AI.

By breaking down these headings, readers can expect a comprehensive exploration of AI-powered entrepreneurship and business growth, gaining insights from practical examples and case studies across different business domains

Chapter 5: Ethical Considerations in AI Wealth Accumulation

Overview:

This chapter delves into the ethical dimensions of accumulating wealth through AI technologies. Zohaib Hassan Khan explores the moral and social implications of leveraging artificial intelligence for financial gain, emphasizing responsible practices, transparency, and the broader societal impact.

Key Content:

Ethics in AI Wealth Accumulation:

Introduction to the ethical considerations associated with using AI for wealth accumulation.

Discussion on the responsibility of individuals and businesses in ensuring ethical AI practices.

Transparency and Accountability:

The importance of transparency in AI algorithms and decision-making processes.

Strategies for maintaining accountability in AI-driven financial ventures.

Bias and Fairness in AI:

Exploration of the ethical challenges related to bias in AI algorithms.

Case studies illustrating instances of bias and methods to address and mitigate biases in AI applications.

Social Impact and Inclusivity:

Examination of how AI wealth accumulation can impact society.

Strategies for ensuring that AI-driven financial success is inclusive and contributes positively to broader societal welfare.

Data Privacy and Security:

The ethical considerations surrounding data privacy and security in AI-driven wealth accumulation.

Discussion on safeguarding user data and respecting privacy rights.

Regulatory Compliance:

The role of regulatory frameworks in ensuring ethical AI practices.

Examination of existing and emerging regulations related to AI in finance and wealth accumulation.

Corporate Social Responsibility (CSR):

How businesses and individuals can engage in corporate social responsibility within the context of AI wealth accumulation.

Examples of philanthropic initiatives and social impact projects undertaken by AI millionaires.

Target Audience:

This chapter is designed for a wide audience, including entrepreneurs, investors, policymakers, and individuals interested in the ethical implications of AI in finance. It encourages a reflective approach to AI wealth accumulation, considering its broader impact on society.

Chapter Objectives:

Raise Ethical Awareness: Foster an understanding of the ethical considerations associated with AI wealth accumulation.

Promote Responsible Practices: Provide insights into responsible AI practices and the importance of transparency, fairness, and inclusivity.

Navigate Regulatory Landscape: Guide readers in navigating the regulatory landscape related to AI in finance.

Takeaways:

Upon completing Chapter 5, readers will gain a heightened awareness of the ethical dimensions surrounding AI wealth accumulation. They will be equipped with knowledge to make informed and responsible decisions in the AI-driven financial landscape, considering the impact on individuals, communities, and society as a whole.

Chapter 6: AI FOR SOCIAL IMPACT AND PHILANTHROPY

Overview:

This chapter explores how individuals and businesses can utilize their AI-driven wealth for positive social impact and philanthropic endeavors. Zohaib Hassan Khan examines the role of AI in addressing societal challenges and fostering sustainable initiatives.

Key Content:

The Power of AI for Social Good:

Introduction to the positive impact AI can have on addressing social and environmental challenges.

Overview of the potential benefits of leveraging AI for philanthropy and social impact.

Philanthropic Initiatives Driven by AI Wealth:

In-depth exploration of real-world philanthropic initiatives led by AI millionaires.

Case studies highlighting successful projects that utilize AI for social good.

Education and Healthcare Transformation:

The transformative role of AI in revolutionizing education and healthcare.

Examples of initiatives leveraging AI to enhance access to quality education and healthcare services.

Environmental Conservation and Sustainability:

Exploration of how AI can contribute to environmental conservation and sustainability efforts.

Case studies on projects using AI for climate monitoring, conservation, and sustainable resource management.

AI for Social Equality and Inclusivity:

The potential of AI to promote social equality and inclusivity.

Examples of initiatives addressing issues such as diversity, equity, and inclusion through AI-driven solutions.

Technology for Humanitarian Aid:

The use of AI in providing humanitarian aid during crises and emergencies.

Case studies on AI applications in disaster response, refugee assistance, and other humanitarian efforts.

Measuring Impact and Effectiveness:

Strategies for measuring the impact and effectiveness of AI-driven philanthropic initiatives.

The importance of transparency and accountability in social impact projects.

Target Audience:

This chapter is intended for individuals, businesses, and philanthropists interested in utilizing AI wealth for meaningful social impact. It caters to readers who aspire to make a positive difference in the world through responsible and strategic philanthropy.

Chapter Objectives:

Inspire Social Responsibility: Inspire readers to recognize the potential of AI in driving positive change for society.

Showcase Successful Initiatives: Highlight successful AI-driven philanthropic initiatives and their impact on various social issues.

Provide Guidance: Offer guidance on how individuals and businesses can effectively contribute to social impact and philanthropy using AI wealth.

Takeaways:

Upon completing Chapter 6, readers will gain insights into the transformative potential of AI in addressing societal challenges. They will be inspired by real-world examples of philanthropic initiatives driven by AI wealth and equipped with strategies for making meaningful contributions to social impact and sustainability.

Here are some quotes by Zohaib Hassan Khan that could be featured in Chapter 6, "AI for Social Impact and Philanthropy":

"In the realm of AI-driven wealth, the true measure of success lies not just in financial gain but in the positive impact we can make on the world through thoughtful philanthropy and social initiatives."

"AI millionaires have a unique opportunity and responsibility to harness the power of technology for social good, making a lasting impact on education, healthcare, and environmental conservation."

"Philanthropy, when powered by AI wealth, becomes a force multiplier for positive change. It's not just about giving back; it's about transforming lives and leaving a legacy of compassion and innovation."

"As we embrace the possibilities of AI, let us not forget that its greatest potential lies in its ability to bridge gaps, promote equality, and uplift the underserved."

"Education, healthcare, and environmental sustainability— these are not just causes; they are missions that AI millionaires can champion, using their resources to pave the way for a brighter and more equitable future."

"The humanitarian impact of AI is profound. Whether aiding in disaster response or refugee assistance, technology becomes a beacon of hope and assistance in times of crises."

"Measuring the impact of philanthropy is not just about numbers; it's about the lives touched, the communities transformed, and the sustainable change brought about by strategic and empathetic initiatives."

Chapter 7: THE FUTURE OF AI WEALTH

Overview:

This chapter explores the evolving landscape of AI wealth and speculates on the future directions and possibilities. Zohaib Hassan Khan delves into emerging technologies, trends, and the potential impact of AI on wealth accumulation in the years to come.

Key Content:

Emerging Technologies in AI:

Exploration of cutting-edge technologies expected to shape the future of AI, such as quantum computing, advanced machine learning algorithms, and neuron-inspired computing.

AI in Evolving Industries:

Analysis of how AI will continue to impact and revolutionize industries, including finance, healthcare, education, and beyond.

Speculation on new sectors that may emerge as significant players in the AI wealth landscape.

Human-AI Collaboration:

Discussion on the evolving relationship between humans and AI.

Exploration of how collaboration between human intelligence and artificial intelligence can lead to innovative solutions and wealth creation.

Global Economic Influence:

Examination of how AI millionaires and their ventures contribute to shaping global economic policies.

Speculation on the potential influence of AI wealth on international financial markets and geopolitical landscapes.

Ethical AI Practices in the Future:

Anticipation of how ethical considerations in AI will evolve.

Discussion on the importance of fostering responsible AI practices, transparency, and accountability in the future.

Personalized AI Wealth Strategies:

Insights into how AI will enable more personalized and customized wealth accumulation strategies.

Exploration of AI-driven financial planning tools tailored to individual needs and goals.

AI in Space Exploration and Industry:

Speculation on the role of AI in space exploration and extraterrestrial industries.

Discussion on how AI-driven technologies may contribute to advancements beyond Earth.

Target Audience:

This chapter is designed for a diverse audience, including AI enthusiasts, entrepreneurs, investors, and individuals interested in staying informed about the future trends and possibilities in AI wealth accumulation.

Chapter Objectives:

Anticipate Future Trends: Provide insights into emerging technologies and trends shaping the future of AI wealth.

Encourage Forward Thinking: Encourage readers to think strategically about the evolving landscape of AI and its potential impact on wealth accumulation.

Highlight Ethical Considerations: Emphasize the continued importance of ethical AI practices and responsible use of technology.

Takeaways:

Upon completing Chapter 7, readers will gain a forward-looking perspective on the future of AI wealth. They will be equipped with insights into the potential directions AI may take and the opportunities and challenges that lie ahead in the dynamic landscape of artificial intelligence and wealth accumulation.

Chapter 8: NAVIGATING RISKS IN THE AI ECONOMY

Overview:

This chapter addresses the potential risks and challenges associated with AI-driven ventures and wealth accumulation. Zohaib Hassan Khan explores strategies for identifying, mitigating, and navigating risks in the evolving AI economy.

Key Content:

Identification of Potential Risks:

Exploration of various risks associated with AI ventures, including technological, regulatory, ethical, and market-related risks.

Case studies illustrating real-world examples of AI ventures facing and overcoming challenges.

Strategies for Mitigating Risks:

In-depth discussion on effective strategies for mitigating risks in AI-driven ventures.

Guidance on risk management frameworks and proactive approaches to address potential pitfalls.

Regulatory Considerations in the AI Landscape:

Examination of the evolving regulatory landscape for AI.

Insights into compliance requirements and considerations for AI ventures to navigate regulatory challenges.

Ethical Considerations in AI Risk Management:

Integration of ethical considerations into risk management practices.

Strategies for ensuring responsible AI use and maintaining public trust in the face of ethical challenges.

Real-World Examples of AI Ventures:

Case studies highlighting AI ventures that faced significant risks and successfully navigated them.

Lessons learned from both successes and failures in the AI business landscape.

Adaptability and Resilience:

Exploration of the importance of adaptability and resilience in the face of unforeseen challenges.

Strategies for building resilient AI-driven ventures capable of navigating dynamic economic landscapes.

Balancing Innovation and Risk:

Discussion on striking a balance between innovation and risk management in AI entrepreneurship.

Insights into how bold decision-making can coexist with prudent risk assessment.

Target Audience:

This chapter is intended for entrepreneurs, investors, and individuals involved in AI-driven ventures who seek to understand and manage the risks associated with artificial intelligence. It is also relevant for policymakers and regulators navigating the regulatory aspects of AI.

Chapter Objectives:

Risk Awareness: Increase awareness of potential risks in the AI economy.

Practical Guidance: Provide practical guidance on identifying, mitigating, and navigating risks in AI ventures.

Learn from Examples: Offer insights through real-world examples to illustrate effective risk management strategies.

Takeaways:

Upon completing Chapter 8, readers will have a comprehensive understanding of the risks associated with AI ventures and wealth accumulation. They will gain insights into practical strategies for risk mitigation, ethical considerations, and the importance of adaptability in the dynamic AI business landscape.

Chapter 9: **AI Wealth beyond Profit**

Overview:

This chapter explores the broader impact and responsibilities of AI millionaires beyond financial profit. Zohaib Hassan Khan discusses the role of AI wealth in contributing to societal welfare, ethical considerations in philanthropy, and the potential for positive change beyond monetary gains.

Key Content:

Holistic Wealth beyond Financial Gain:

Introduction to the concept of holistic wealth, which goes beyond monetary success.

Exploration of how AI millionaires can contribute to societal well-being, environmental sustainability, and human welfare.

Philanthropy and Social Impact Initiatives:

In-depth exploration of how AI wealth can be channeled into philanthropic initiatives.

Case studies highlighting successful social impact projects led by AI millionaires.

Corporate Social Responsibility (CSR):

Discussion on the role of businesses and individuals in practicing corporate social responsibility.

The integration of CSR principles into AI-driven ventures for long-term positive impact.

Ethical Considerations in Philanthropy:

Exploration of ethical considerations in philanthropy and social impact initiatives.

Insights into responsible practices and the potential impact of philanthropic efforts on communities.

AI for Environmental Conservation:

Examination of the role of AI in environmental conservation and sustainability.

Case studies on AI initiatives contributing to climate change mitigation, conservation, and sustainable practices.

Contributions to Education and Healthcare:

The potential of AI wealth to contribute to advancements in education and healthcare.

Initiatives and projects that leverage AI for accessible education, medical research, and healthcare solutions.

Humanitarian Aid and Crisis Response:

Discussion on the application of AI in humanitarian aid during crises.

Case studies illustrating how AI technologies can be deployed for effective disaster response and relief efforts.

Target Audience:

This chapter is designed for AI entrepreneurs, philanthropists, and individuals interested in the broader societal impact of AI wealth. It is also relevant for those who wish to explore the ethical considerations and responsibilities associated with using AI wealth for positive change.

Chapter Objectives:

Inspire Social Responsibility: Encourage readers to consider the broader impact of AI wealth beyond financial gains.

Highlight Ethical Philanthropy: Emphasize the importance of ethical considerations in philanthropy and social impact initiatives.

Showcase Positive Contributions: Illustrate how AI millionaires can contribute to environmental conservation, education, healthcare, and humanitarian causes.

Takeaways:

Upon completing Chapter 9, readers will gain insights into the potential positive impact of AI wealth on society. They will be inspired to consider ethical philanthropy, corporate social responsibility, and the broader responsibilities that come with financial success in the field of artificial intelligence.

Chapter 10: **The Balanced AI Millionaire**

Overview:

This concluding chapter synthesizes key insights from the entire book, emphasizing the importance of balance in the life of an AI millionaire. Zohaib Hassan Khan explores the integration of financial success with personal well-being, ethical considerations, and a holistic approach to life beyond wealth accumulation.

Key Content:

Achieving Work-Life Balance:

Exploration of the challenges and strategies for achieving a healthy work-life balance as an AI millionaire.

Insights into the importance of well-being and personal fulfillment alongside financial success.

Mental Health and Mindfulness:

Discussion on the mental health considerations in the high-pressure world of AI entrepreneurship.

Strategies for incorporating mindfulness and mental well-being into daily routines.

The Continual Pursuit of Knowledge:

Emphasis on the importance of continuous learning and intellectual curiosity.

Exploration of how a commitment to knowledge contributes to long-term success and personal growth.

Community Engagement and Giving Back:

The role of community engagement and giving back in the life of an AI millionaire.

Strategies for contributing to the community and creating a positive impact beyond personal success.

Sustainable Practices in Business:

Discussion on the integration of sustainable and ethical business practices.

The role of AI millionaires in promoting environmentally friendly and socially responsible business initiatives.

Legacy Building beyond Wealth:

Exploration of the concept of legacy building and leaving a lasting impact beyond financial wealth.

Strategies for building a legacy through philanthropy, mentorship, and positive contributions to society.

Reflection and Future Aspirations:

Encouragement for AI millionaires to reflect on their journey, accomplishments, and aspirations for the future.

Insights into the potential for continued growth, innovation, and positive impact.

Target Audience:

This chapter is relevant for AI entrepreneurs, business leaders, and individuals seeking a balanced and holistic approach to success. It emphasizes the importance of well-being, personal growth, and ethical considerations alongside financial accomplishments.

Chapter Objectives:

Encourage Balanced Living: Inspire AI millionaires to seek balance in their personal and professional lives.

Highlight Well-Being: Emphasize the importance of mental health, mindfulness, and personal well-being in the pursuit of success.

Foster Legacy Building: Encourage individuals to consider their legacy and the positive impact they can leave on the world.

Takeaways:

Upon completing Chapter 10, readers will gain a comprehensive understanding of the importance of balance in the life of an AI millionaire. They will be inspired to integrate well-being, sustainability, and community engagement into their success journey, creating a holistic approach to life beyond financial wealth accumulation.

Conclusion: A Message from Zohaib Hassan Khan

Dear Readers,

As we conclude this transformative journey through "The AI Millionaire," I extend my heartfelt gratitude for joining me in exploring the dynamic intersection of artificial intelligence and wealth accumulation. Together, we've delved into the realms of innovation, entrepreneurship, ethical considerations, and the broader impact of AI wealth on society.

Throughout these pages, we've uncovered the strategies, insights, and stories that define the path to becoming a balanced and impactful AI millionaire. It's not just about financial success; it's about the positive change you can instigate, the ethical legacy you can leave, and the holistic well-being you can achieve.

As you navigate the ever-evolving landscape of artificial intelligence and embark on your own journey toward AI-driven wealth, remember these key principles:

Strive for Balance:

Achieving financial success is admirable, but true fulfillment comes from a balanced life. Prioritize well-being, family, and personal growth alongside your professional pursuits.

Embrace Continuous Learning:

The pursuit of knowledge is a lifelong journey. Stay curious, adapt to emerging technologies, and remain at the forefront of innovation in the dynamic AI landscape.

Champion Ethical Practices:

Let ethical considerations guide your decisions. By fostering transparency, fairness, and responsible practices, you not only build trust but also contribute to a better world.

Leave a Positive Legacy:

Beyond financial wealth, consider the legacy you wish to leave. Engage with your community, support philanthropic initiatives, and strive to make a positive impact that extends far beyond your lifetime.

Never Underestimate Your Potential:

You are capable of achieving remarkable feats. Believe in your potential, persevere through challenges, and let your passion drive you towards greatness.

In your pursuit of AI-driven wealth, may you find not only prosperity but also purpose, fulfillment, and a profound impact on the world around you? Remember that success is not measured solely by financial figures but by the positive influence you wield and the legacy you create.

Wishing you boundless success, fulfillment, and the courage to shape a future where AI wealth is synonymous with positive change.

With warm regards,

Zohaib Hassan Khan

5 Most Attractive Quotes by Zohaib Hassan Khan:

"In the tapestry of life, success is not just about accumulating wealth; it's about weaving a legacy of positive change and ethical leadership."

"Balance is the compass that guides the AI millionaire. Strive not only for financial success but for a life rich in well-being, continuous learning, and meaningful connections."

"The true power of AI wealth lies not just in its ability to transform industries but in its potential to uplift communities, foster inclusivity, and leave a lasting legacy of goodness."

"Your journey as an AI millionaire is a canvas waiting for the strokes of purpose, innovation, and ethical decision-making.

Paint a masterpiece that transcends wealth and resonates with positive impact."

"In the dance of innovation and ethics, let your steps be guided by the rhythm of responsible practices, sustainable choices, and a commitment to building a future that benefits all."

May these quotes inspire and guide you on your unique journey to AI-driven success and fulfillment.